# Haywards Heath
## Past and Present

Dick Turpin's Cottage, on the corner of Boltro Road and Paddockhall Road, was demolished in 1887 and the police station built on its site

## Lilian Rogers

### Photography: David Brook

#### S.B. Publications

**Dedicated to:**
Joan and John Norman, to whom I owe
such a large debt of gratitude

By the same author
*Yesterday and Today,* 1987
*The Story of Haywards Heath,* 1998, with Wyn Ford
*Haywards Heath, Yesterday Remembered,* 1999

First published in 2002 by S B Publications
19 Grove Road, Seaford, Sussex BN25 1TP
telephone: 01323 893498
fax: 01323 893860
email: sales@sbpublications.swinternet.co.uk

© 2002 Lilian Rogers
The moral right of the author has been asserted

ISBN 185770 264 6

ERRATUM
Page 65 should read: The Cuckfield rural district council offices built in 1901 were demolished to be replaced by an office block in 1987.

Typeset by JEM Editorial, jemedit@aol.com
Printed and bound by Tansleys Printers, Seaford, East Sussex
01323 891019

Front cover picture:   Sussex Square, early nineteenth century
Back cover picture:    America Lane about 100 years ago

# CONTENTS

| | |
|---|---|
| Foreword from the Mayor of Haywards Heath | 4 |
| Introduction | 5 |
| South Road | 7 |
| Sussex Square | 22 |
| Sussex Road | 30 |
| Wivelsfield Road | 37 |
| Fox Hill | 38 |
| Colwell Road | 39 |
| Franklynn Road | 40 |
| Hazelgrove Road | 44 |
| New England Road | 45 |
| Bentswood | 48 |
| America Lane | 49 |
| Oathall Road | 50 |
| Sydney Road | 53 |
| Millgreen Road | 54 |
| Barnmead | 56 |
| Harlands Farm | 57 |
| Market Place | 58 |
| Market Place and Railway Approach | 60 |
| Lucastes Avenue | 61 |
| Boltro Road | 62 |
| The Broadway | 67 |
| Perrymount Road | 74 |
| Clair Road | 81 |
| Commercial Square | 83 |
| Church Road | 85 |
| Muster Green | 87 |
| Butlers Green | 92 |
| Transport in Haywards Heath | 93 |
| About the author | 96 |

Acknowledgements and thanks are due to: Irene Balls, Donald Barnes, Phyll Chappell, Dianne Jones, Dave Tucker, Rebecca Vernum-Holder, John Norman – and to Channel Photography for the Bentswood picture.

# FOREWORD

The ever-changing face and character of Haywards Heath are brought into sharp definition by Lilian Rogers' fascinating portrayal of the town past and present.

The author's striking collection of time-contrasting photographs invites reflection upon the dramatic effect of decades of development and modernisation. Time never stands still.

Sheep no longer graze in the meadow that is now Victoria Park, nor do gaggles of noisy geese traverse Sussex Square, where children once played in safety. The Haywards Heath of today plays host to the railway and cars – its urban lifestyle so different from its rural past.

This book achieves that precious sense of connection, continuity and place – all good fuel to stimulate debate as Haywards Heath develops its plans for the future.

**Irene Balls**
**Mayor of Haywards Heath**
**2002**

# INTRODUCTION

In the past different people have had different notions regarding the derivation of the town's name. Today we know that here was once the Manor of Heyworth, and it is believed that the now demolished Great Haywards was the manor house, and Little Haywards a subsidiary farm, the house remaining in Haywards Road. Some land of the manor was not suitable for cultivation and was known as 'waste of the manor' – a heath or, in the local dialect, a 'hothe'. Thus Heyworth's heath became Haywards Heath and some of that heath has been intentionally retained in the Heath Recreation Ground.

There were several tracks throughout, linking scattered farm cottages and houses, some long demolished, but others remain. Little Haywards in Haywards Road dates from $c$1400; in Butlers Green Road, Steeple Cottage is shown on the 1638 manorial map, but is probably older. Boultrowe farm house, standing today as The Old House, on the top corner of Boltro Road, dates from the sixteenth century; Lucas's, now Lucas House in Lucastes Avenue, dates back to the sixteenth century; Muster House on Muster Green, originally smaller, is $c$1750 – and there are others.

A windmill with its adjoining miller's house was standing almost opposite where St Wilfrid's Church was sited, and the millstone on the Muster Green is purported to have come from there. In the 1629 beating of the bounds, a water mill is mentioned; while Bridger's farm, mill, and a piece of land with a windmill, was being offered for sale in an 1800 *Sussex Weekly Advertiser*. There was a tollgate and tollhouse at the upper end of Rocky Lane, and another at Butlers Green.

Then in 1837 the London, Brighton and South Coast Railway secured a strip of land across Haywards Heath, and on July 12, 1841, the line from the capital to Haywards Heath was opened and the last part of the track to Brighton completed four months later, reducing much farmland.

In 1861, 159 acres of heath were enclosed; Muster Green was to be kept for public use and a part designated for the building of a church. Until then worship had been in the tiny St Wilfrid's School, and the population of 400 was on the increase. Brighton business people were quick to realise how pleasant it would be to live in this small, quiet, rural locality, and commute to their work places. Houses were built, Haywards Heath had started to grow, and has continued, having today a population figure of 22,685.

The following pages will give an indication of how the town has grown and altered. Those who have lived in Haywards Heath for many years can, indeed, say with William Wordsworth:

> *It is not now as it hath been of yore;*
> *Turn wheresoe'er I may,*
> *By night or day*
> *The things which I have seen I now can see no more.*

**Lilian Rogers**
**Haywards Heath**
**2002**

# SOUTH ROAD

Opened in 1857, St Wilfrid's School was also used for worship, being known as the Chapel School until 1865, when the church was built. There were additions made before a move to Eastern Road in 1951. Today, Zizzi's restaurant is seen in the front, the Christian Science church at the rear.

# SOUTH ROAD

From where the National Westminster bank now stands and along to the park was Stanford Place, with one butcher's shop, the remainder, houses. Offices and businesses have taken their place and Stanford Place is now part of South Road.

## SOUTH ROAD

One addition to St Wilfrid's School was built along South Road's frontage, and after demolition became in 1959 the shops seen today as Park Parade.

# SOUTH ROAD

The Haywards Heath District Council purchased Mr Pannett's meadow in 1897, and as a memorial of the Queen's diamond jubilee, named it Victoria Park. Today we see fewer trees and not a sheep in sight.

## SOUTH ROAD

Next to the park, the council's offices were built in 1903, and housed the fire station, until the offices were moved and the fire station used the whole building. A move for the firemen in 1961 meant demolition for the building in 1981, and on the site the Victoria Gate shops were erected.

## SOUTH ROAD

Haywards Road on the left and a rural view down towards the park; in the road one cyclist, a horse and cart and a man with a barrow. What a contrast today!

## SOUTH ROAD

Mr Sherlock, a seafaring man, lived in Canton Cottage and on his garden built a little model house using sea shells. Today, Lloyds Bank stands on the site.

## SOUTH ROAD

Heathmere, a private residence, later a boys' school, then a pupil teacher centre and finally a county school for girls. It was demolished in 1935 for commercial development.

## SOUTH ROAD

A view looking toward Sussex Square. Heathmere's playing field on the left, houses on the right. In the road, two horses with carts, a parked barrow and a pedestrian, while another two walk on the pavement. More pedestrians and an increase in road traffic today!

## SOUTH ROAD

On that same playing field a council school was built in 1907, Owen Freestone being headmaster from the start to his retirement in 1937. A year later the front part of the school was demolished for commercial development, the rear portion retained for use as workshops.

# SOUTH ROAD

Another view looking down South Road, Pelham Cottages next to George Hilton's shop, and further down, two more shops, a gas lamp-post in place, but, as yet, having no top.

# SOUTH ROAD

A close-up later in the year, for the trees are in leaf; the gas lamp ready for use, and the two shops identified as Miss Robinson's toy shop and Mr Smith's boot and shoe store.

# SOUTH ROAD

The trees have gone, the tall photographic studio taking their place. Displayed in the window, portraits and photographs by Mr Tulett, Mr Banbury and Mr Austen Walters; now, organic food is displayed in the window.

## SOUTH ROAD

Houses, and next to them a plot of land acquired for the building of a Congregational church, which was ready for worship in 1915. It stands today as a United Reformed church, with Woolworths taking the place of the houses.

# SOUTH ROAD

Here, next to the lower edge of the same plot, was Isted's coach works, later H Brown's garage, also a drapery and a dairy, all today part of Boots.

# SUSSEX SQUARE

The terracotta eagle stands high on the roof of the Public Hall, built 1889, having a name change to Sussex Hall after renovation, when the eagle departed. Mr Walder has two ironmongery shops, while parked is a haycart and a car.

## SUSSEX SQUARE

The background of tree-lined South Road presents a rural appearance. In the foreground both Mr and Mrs Uridge have a shop, and it's quite safe for children to play in the centre of the cross-roads.

# SUSSEX SQUARE

Mr Grimsdick is here seen in front of his shop on the Hazelgrove Road corner. Later, with road improvement, the garden disappeared and, in 2001, shop and house were demolished.

## SUSSEX SQUARE

The geese, purchased at the local market, are being driven to a Rocky Lane farm, but not before they were driven over tar, then sand, to protect the webbing on their feet from flint roads. Not advisable to drive geese over Sussex Square today.

25

## SUSSEX SQUARE

A 1974 picture showing the Priory Lodge and a traffic island (its predecessor, wooden and painted white, was nicknamed the Queen Mary). The roundabout was to be installed soon after this picture was taken.

# SUSSEX SQUARE

In the distance a pair of horses pulling a cart, and a mother pushes her pram. The foreground shows two men, a hand-cart, a little manure; and Miss Crichton's corn store is well advertised at Victoria House, on the Gower Road corner.

# SUSSEX SQUARE

The coronation of King George VI, 1937, and the town decorates. The hole is dug; two carpenters have arrived to make a groove in the pole, to hold the rope. The hoisting is taking seven men, three ladders of different lengths and one piece of rope, while an eighth man looks on; so does an old-aged pensioner (no senior citizens yet). The eighth man wasn't just a spectator, he was waiting his turn.

# SUSSEX SQUARE

He's now at the top of the pole securing the rope. A ninth man fixes his end, opposite on the roof. In 2002 a crane in South Road hoists a banner. Much less manpower.

## SUSSEX ROAD

A 1914 picture shows Mrs Harris has a sweet shop, Mr Harris is in business as a fruiterer and greengrocer, the Co-Operative Society has expanded from one to two shops, and Piper's clothing mart stands on the corner, well advertised.

# SUSSEX ROAD

Royal Cottages, demolished for shops in 1977, stands next to a Methodist church, 1877-1991, becoming a Baptist church in 1994. The former Royal Cottages are now shops.

## SUSSEX ROAD

Two soldiers crossing the road give a possible dating of 1914-1918; trees are growing on the shops' frontages, and what a rural view Hazelgrove Road presents.

# SUSSEX ROAD

Houses on the right hand side, but on the opposite side Mr Brown's paper shop, and one of his placards may give a probable date of 1926, as it states: '25,000 miners strike today'. Alma Cottages stand next to the shop, their name linking their age to the Crimean War.

# SUSSEX ROAD

Heath Cottages, built 1884, but in one, Mr Scutt is selling teas, cold ham, ices, minerals, all at the Sussex Road Confectionary. They are today numbers 26 and 28, and selling pine furniture.

# SUSSEX ROAD

At Waterloo House on Triangle Road corner, James Box had a butcher's shop and adjoining it a grocery, all within living memory, but in this 1912 picture he is seen as a florist and nurseryman in both shops.

## SUSSEX ROAD

The number of pedestrians adds up to six boys, three on the pavement, three on the road, while traffic on that road shows a hand cart; rather busier today.

# WIVELSFIELD ROAD

The New Inn, later known as the Ugly Duckling, and standing today as The Duck, now minus its adjoining house.

# FOX HILL

The Fox and Hounds at the lower end of Fox Hill was an old coaching inn, shown here with two coach houses and advertising good stabling. The 1861 census gives the landlord as a farmer of twenty-four acres, so it would seem probable that the inn stood on that farmland.

# COLWELL ROAD

Built on farmland in 1859, the asylum became St Francis Hospital in 1948. It had two landmarks, one the 120ft boilerhouse chimney, removed in 1975, another the water tower, still there. After closure in 1995 the Grade II Listed building was converted into the Southdowns Park residential development.

# FRANKLYNN ROAD

Birch House was built in 1887 for Mr Jowers, a surgeon, who reckoned to reach the station every morning in eight minutes. Birch House became the Birch Hotel, and a filling station stands where once were the stables for the horses that enabled him to make that daily run.

# FRANKLYNN ROAD

Petlands Farm House, known locally as Fiddle Botting's Cottage, was demolished in 1935 for the Dellney Avenue seen today.

# FRANKLYNN ROAD

The baker's shop with bakery stood on the corner of Franklynn and Triangle Roads, demolished for sheltered accommodation. On its turret today stands a weathervane depicting a baker in long coat and floppy hat offering a tray of bread rolls, the work of Ben Autie, a Lewes blacksmith.

# FRANKLYNN ROAD

The Priory of Our Lady of Good Counsel was built in stages between 1887 and 1898 on Hazelgrove Park. A move to Sayers Common in 1978 left the listed building to become offices and a restaurant, its fourteen acres for housing; the first residents arrived in 1972.

# HAZELGROVE ROAD

Lyntonville and five other houses in Hazelgrove Road were demolished in 1982 for a car park to serve the new shopping precinct.

# NEW ENGLAND ROAD

The council yard, top right, and children stand in the road. Today is seen Mayflower Court, and it would not be wise to stand in the road.

45

# NEW ENGLAND ROAD

The Presentation Church, an iron building from 1882 until 1897, when a brick-built church was erected, the former building then becoming a parish room, and used as a Sunday school. After the parish room was destroyed by fire in 1979, a new hall was built in 1983.

# NEW ENGLAND ROAD

View from New England Road, Haywards Heath.

A view from New England Road into Petlands Wood, where it would seem a gate had previously enclosed the track that was to become Western Road, with the cemetery now down in the dip.

# BENTSWOOD

A lovely wood with footpaths from New England and Oathall Roads, the latter where now is Oathall Avenue. The first council-owned houses were built in 1924 in New England Road, followed by those in Mayflower Road and Woodlands Road, until Mr Bent's wood was taken for further development.

# AMERICA LANE

This is where William Allen established his colony in 1825 on the Gravelye Estate, then in Lindfield; some houses were thatched, some slate-roofed. In 1937 a demolition order was made, and the whole area is now developed.

# OATHALL ROAD

Farlington, a school for girls, was founded in 1896 in Farlington House. A move made to Strood Park, Horsham, left a twelve-acre site for the building of Farlington Close and Farlington Avenue in 1955.

# OATHALL ROAD

Another school stood next to Farlington, a preparatory school for boys, Brunswick. Upon its site today stands St Paul's Roman Catholic College, built in 1964.

# OATHALL ROAD

A view of the lower part of the road, *c*1911, with no traffic, paved one side only, and, on the right side, trees where today houses stand.

# SYDNEY ROAD

Southlands Farm, with an early mention of 1638, in what was to become Sydney Road, near Church Avenue. By 1890 it had been broken up, and its pond filled in.

The Chapel of the Holy Spirit, erected in 1897, was in the same ecclesiastical parish as the church of St Wilfrid, becoming a separate one in 1916, with its name changed to St Richard. The present one was built in 1938, nearby, both standing on the farm's site.

# MILLGREEN ROAD

A 1912 view of the road; on the opposite side stood a second gasholder. In 1961 the fire station moved from South Road to this site.

# MILLGREEN ROAD

The Millgreen Road and College Road corner, showing both the rurality and urbanity, as the two roads of houses meet the cornfield of Wickham Farm. The site today is taken by the Mid-Sussex Timber Company.

# BARNMEAD

Bridger's Mill was built in 1840, and shown on the 1874 Ordnance Survey map as being in an isolated position. It was demolished in 1968, its millpond drained and filled in, for the Barnmead development, though the stream still flows underground in a culvert, emerging at Millgreen Road.

# HARLANDS FARM

Harlands Farm dates back to the sixteenth century and may have been larger than its sixty-eight acres mentioned in a 1964 bill of sale. The house remains, but two schools, offices, houses and the Dolphin Leisure Centre have claimed the farmland.

# MARKET PLACE

The market opened in 1866 and finished trading in 1990, its seven acre site being acquired for a Sainsbury's supermarket, which opened in 1991.

## MARKET PLACE

Caffyns Garage replaced four cottages, 1-4 Market Place, and both the horse trough and Southdown buses have gone, while Harlands Road and Radnor House stand where once was part of the market.

# MARKET PLACE AND RAILWAY APPROACH

The main entrance to the railway station prior to 1933 was here, and seen above it, the stationmaster's house, while the tall building next to it was a corn store for Bridger's Mill, destroyed by fire in 1915.

# LUCASTES AVENUE

Not a lot going on here; but something is afoot, for drainage pipes are at the ready, and twenty-seven building sites were being auctioned there in 1902. Any resident of Lucas's would have walked the track for the house was built in the 1500s, standing today as Lucas House.

# BOLTRO ROAD

The police station built in 1887 had a courthouse added a year later, and later still, in 1937, a children's court. A move in 1992 took station and court house to the corner of Bolnore Road, and the former building was demolished in 1999. Part of Charter Gate now stands on the site.

# BOLTRO ROAD

The first main post office was at Muster House, the second at The Yews in Boltro Road; this picture shows the third, built in 1894. After post office use, it served as a telephone exchange before becoming a sorting office. It was demolished in 1998 and the site is now used for Charter Gate flats.

# BOLTRO ROAD

The fourth post office on the opposite side of the road was erected in 1915, and served until 1986 with a move to the Orchards shopping centre. It was demolished in 1995, and on its site stands office development housing the Jobcentre.

# BOLTRO ROAD

The Cuckfield Road district council offices built in 1901 were demolished to be replaced by an office block in 1987.

# BOLTRO ROAD

An office block also replaces Albion House, which served as offices for the Mid-Sussex District Council, before being demolished in 1987.

# THE BROADWAY

The upper part of The Broadway down to the road over the tunnel was Clifton Place, with Clifton Villas, Clifton Terrace and Clifton House. Here is seen a beer house advertising 'Fine Old Mild and Bitter Ales', a small shop is attached.

# THE BROADWAY

The little shop gone, the Star Hotel replaces the beer house and the path is paved and curbed.

## THE BROADWAY

In the background is Mr Alwenn's butcher's shop in Standford Place, later to become Mr Pratt's butcher's shop in South Road. Clifton House is a chemist's owned by Mr Hayes, later Mr Dixon. The path on the left is not curbed and grass grows in the gutter.

# THE BROADWAY

Coventry Buildings sweep around the corner of Church Road and the Broadway – no longer Clifton Place. Mr Hampton has a cycle shop and a motor garage.

## THE BROADWAY

The Coventry Motor Works was later to become Caffyns Garage. The private residence next to the garage was, for forty years, Michael Denman's photographic shop, and is now Park Cameras.

# THE BROADWAY

Ardlin House was demolished for the building of the Haywards Heath Building Society offices in 1938; this was relinquished in 1989. Today it is the Café Rouge.

# THE BROADWAY

The Broadway, 1904, and the tall gabled building, centre left, was Mr Wood's cycle and motor business. With his departure the building was converted into a cinema, the Heath Theatre, which opened in 1911, closing in 1932. On the right was Mr Soper's strawberry garden, taken today by shops.

# PERRYMOUNT ROAD

At the top end of the road was the Broadway Cinema, opening in 1932, the first show beginning with a selection played by the Haywards Heath Town Band. Its closure came in 1952, when it was adapted as furniture showrooms for JW Upton and Sons, and demolished for offices in 1987.

# PERRYMOUNT ROAD

Below the cinema were houses, and many were to go in the 1980s. Here are car showrooms, shops and a house, The Nutshell, all demolished for an office block in 1981.

## PERRYMOUNT ROAD

A rural view before the bank was crazy-paved and houses behind the trees demolished, their names but memories – San Remo, St Hilda, Portresina, Heathfield, Shortfield.

# PERRYMOUNT ROAD

Built as a Wesleyan church in 1900, today it is the Haywards Heath Methodist Church, and in 2001-2 underwent extensive refurbishment for both worship and community needs.

# PERRYMOUNT ROAD

St Clair Meadow was opened as a children's play area in 1935 and served as such until 1974 when Clair Hall was built on the site.

# PERRYMOUNT ROAD

Jesse Finch, one of the town's early builders, had his workshops on the lower corner, where a bus station was built in 1954, closing in 1980. The building remains as offices.

# PERRYMOUNT ROAD

The Perrymount Cinema with dance hall and café-restaurant opened in 1936, and despite more than 1,000 signatures to keep it open, closed in 1972, being demolished in 1984. In 1996 its site was to become the entrance to an office block, Sussex House.

# CLAIR ROAD

On the corner of Clair Road and Perrymount Road stood a filling station, where Cleveland flats were erected in 1989.

# CLAIR ROAD

At the lower end of Clair Road stood the Liverpool Hotel, beginning its life as a beer house with the coming of the railway in 1841, and later in the 1920s changing its name to the Liverpool Arms. It closed in 1991 and was demolished in 1997 for a fifty-space car park.

## COMMERCIAL SQUARE

An empty square save for one pedestrian outside the Sussex Emporium kept by Mr Beeny, and a horse and cart on the corner of his property. Millgreen Road has a small butcher's shop.

# COMMERCIAL SQUARE

An 1886 picture of the Burrell Arms where Frederick Ferguson is licensee, having taken over in 1878. Jesse Finch's Scandinavian timber-racks stood where now is the railway station, and a second timber yard opposite, where a garage now stands.

# CHURCH ROAD

Richard Pannett stands by his builders' yard next to his home, Highland House. The yard was sold in 1894, and the workshop demolished, leaving a garden and tennis court, until Highland Court flats were built in the 1960s.

## CHURCH ROAD

Trevelyan, a school for girls, founded in the late 1800s, closed in 1966, though it was not demolished until 1985, when the flats Trevelyan Place were erected on the site.

## MUSTER GREEN

A view approaching the green, where through the gate were Coleman's Riding Stables and at the rear of the Star public house, Clevelands Cottages. St Wilfrid's Church tower has no clock, that came in 1921, as the town's peace memorial.

## MUSTER GREEN

Opposite, near the tunnel air shaft, Clevelands, smaller than shown here, was built *c*1840, and demolished for Muster Court flats in 1959.

# MUSTER GREEN

A gas lamp-post, two paths but no flower beds as seen today, and no war memorial until 1924. The memorial, weighing between seven and eight tons, stands 9ft 6in high, and was unveiled at the western end of the green.

89

# MUSTER GREEN

Muster House, since enlarged from when it was built c1750, was the home of Haywards Heath's first post office; the words are discernable above the flat-topped tree, the post office standing close to the horse's head. It was 8ft square. The precinct post office today is larger.

# MUSTER GREEN

Elfinsward, on the corner of Bolnore Road and Butlers Green Road, was a private residence until given to the Chichester diocese for use as a retreat and conference centre, and remained so until demolished in 1970. Today the police station and magistrates' court stand on the site.

# BUTLERS GREEN

In the background stands the house Bolnore, still there today as apartments. On its grounds rises Bolnore Village, in three phases, the first being launched in 1999. The village will occupy 150 acres, of which only forty-five acres are being used for housing.

## TRANSPORT IN HAYWARDS HEATH

Oscar Morison, Howard Pixton and EC Gordon England were three pioneer airmen, the latter living at Oakwood. Sometimes they landed safely, but not on May 9, 1911.

A busy man, Samuel Barnes, for he was also a coal and wood merchant, running his businesses in Wivelsfield Road.

Mr Walder, with a dairy in Sussex Road, seen here probably having collected milk from a farm.

# TRANSPORT IN HAYWARDS HEATH

Mr G Hope, oil and soap merchant, of Big Penny's, Wivelsfield Road, would have had his regular customers.

Jesse Finch, one of the town's early builders, seen here with his wife outside their home, Twyford, in Queen's Road.

Mr G Hilton, with a South Road shop for furniture, soft furnishing – the picture says it all.

## TRANSPORT IN HAYWARDS HEATH

A brand new steam train engine, bearing the town's name.

The horse bus seen here at Bolney conveyed passengers between Bolney, Cuckfield and Haywards Heath; and the local pick-up point was in Market Place.

The driver sits at the wheel of the Mid-Sussex Motor Syndicate's bus, while the conductor stands in front. It ran between Cuckfield, Haywards Heath and Lindfield.

# TRANSPORT IN HAYWARDS HEATH

A Southdown bus, the company being formed in 1915. This one, a number 84, was the town bus.

## ABOUT THE AUTHOR

Lilian Rogers is regarded as Haywards Heath's foremost historian. Apart from wartime service in the WAAF, she has lived in the town all her life and her name is familiar in the *Mid Sussex Times* as the source of many old photographs and postcards. Her first book, *Yesterday Remembered*, proved an instant success. Packed with reminiscences, it is a colourful portrayal of Haywards Heath, reverberating with the people and places she became familiar with as a child growing up in Gower Road.

# Haywards Heath
## Past and Present

Dick Turpin's Cottage, on the corner of Boltro Road and Paddockhall Road, was demolished in 1887 and the police station built on its site

## Lilian Rogers

### Photography: David Brook

S.B. Publications

**Dedicated to:**
Joan and John Norman, to whom I owe
such a large debt of gratitude

By the same author
*Yesterday and Today*, 1987
*The Story of Haywards Heath*, 1998, with Wyn Ford
*Haywards Heath, Yesterday Remembered*, 1999

First published in 2002 by S B Publications
19 Grove Road, Seaford, Sussex BN25 1TP
telephone: 01323 893498
fax: 01323 893860
email: sales@sbpublications.swinternet.co.uk

© 2002 Lilian Rogers
The moral right of the author has been asserted

ISBN 185770 264 6

ERRATUM
Page 65 should read: The Cuckfield rural district council offices
built in 1901 were demolished to be replaced by an office block in 1987.

Typeset by JEM Editorial, jemedit@aol.com
Printed and bound by Tansleys Printers, Seaford, East Sussex
01323 891019

Front cover picture:   Sussex Square, early nineteenth century
Back cover picture:    America Lane about 100 years ago